Nicklaus, Carol.

MUS-BOOK

The picture life of
Cyndi Lauper

10⁰⁰

© THE BAKER & TAYLOR CO.

THE PICTURE LIFE OF CYNDI LAUPER

THE PICTURE LIFE OF

CYNDI LAUPER

BY CAROL NICKLAUS

FRANKLIN WATTS
NEW YORK · LONDON · TORONTO
SYDNEY · 1985

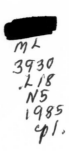
Cover photograph courtesy of
Raeanne Rubenstein

Photographs courtesy of:
Laurie Paladino: pp. 2, 3, 22,
23, 27, 33, 35, 46;
Harry Benson: pp. 6, 45;
Raeanne Rubenstein: pp. 9, 10, 17, 18, 28;
Bill Warren/Gamma Liaison: p. 13;
Ken Walz Productions: pp. 21, 24;
(top) B. Bartholomew/Black Star: p. 31;
(bottom) Alan Tannebaum/Sygma: p. 31;
Bob Riha/Gamma Liaison: p. 32;
UPI/Bettmann Newsphotos: pp. 36, 40, 43;
R. Corkery/Sygma: p. 39;
Michael Jacobs/Sygma: p. 42.

Library of Congress Cataloging in Publication Data

Nicklaus, Carol.
The picture life of Cyndi Lauper.

Summary: Highlights the life and career of the
popular rock singer and video star.
1. Lauper, Cyndi, 1953-   —Juvenile literature.
2. Rock musicians—United States—Biography—Juvenile
literature. [1. Lauper, Cyndi, 1953–   . 2. Singers.
3. Rock music.] I. Title.
ML3930.L18N5 1985   784.5'4'00924 [B] [92]   85-13802
ISBN 0-531-10079-0

THE PICTURE LIFE OF
CYNDI LAUPER

CYNDI LAUPER was born on June 20, 1953. She grew up, with her older sister Elen and younger brother Butch, in the working-class neighborhoods of Williamsburg and Ozone Park in New York City.

Cyndi always had music around her at home. She loved to listen to her mother's records— everything from Louis Armstrong's big band jazz to Eileen Farrell's opera. Cyndi quickly learned the words to popular musical shows, and often entertained her neighbors with her spirited singing.

When Cyndi was five, her parents divorced. After her father left, Cyndi's mother worked long, hard hours as a waitress to support her family. Although it was just across the bridge from the glitter and excitement of Manhattan, life in Ozone Park was not so glamorous.

Cyndi with her mother,
Catrine Domenique,
her grandparents, and
her dog, Sparkle, in
Ozone Park

Cyndi did not want to grow up like all the other girls in Ozone Park. She wanted something different. By the time she was twelve, when most of her schoolmates were trying to be as much like each other as possible, Cyndi was already showing off imaginative, rag-tag outfits she put together herself. Her hair was bright orange. She wore bangles and belts and bracelets and earrings. Dressing up was creative, like her singing, and it was fun. She knew she had talent, and she wanted to express herself.

But school was difficult for Cyndi. She seemed to be a misfit, just by being herself. She didn't do well in the strict environment of the schools she attended. Pursuing her artistic abilities, she studied for a short time at the Fashion Industries High School, but left there as well. Her mother worried. Doing things her own way, Cyndi eventually earned a high school equivalency diploma.

Cyndi has never outgrown her fondness for clothes that set her apart from the crowd.

Cyndi was a teenager during the 1960s, a time that celebrated personal freedom and independence. She listened to the Beatles and the blues. Cyndi learned to play the guitar, and sang folk songs. At seventeen, Cyndi left Ozone Park to find a life of her own. She studied painting with Bob Barrell, an artist who encouraged her in her work, and introduced her to the books of many writers and thinkers. He urged Cyndi to follow her convictions and act on them, whether they were personal, political, or artistic.

Cyndi went north to Canada with her dog, Sparkle, and spent several weeks camping out and painting. But she was a city girl. New York called her back.

Cyndi displays her lesser-known talents on the ukulele during a photo shoot for People magazine.

Cyndi had often been warned by her family and friends about the hardships of a singer's life, but no matter how tough it might be, music was her destiny. She had to give it a try.

By 1975, Cyndi was working the club circuit on Long Island, singing with "cover bands," groups who perform the music of pop stars. After a stint with a band called Doc West, she joined another called Flyer. The work was grueling— long nights prancing and performing songs by Rod Stewart or the Rolling Stones or Janis Joplin, singing at the top of her lungs over the shouts of enthusiastic audiences. Cyndi was at last making music, but it wasn't her own. Her heart wasn't in it. Eventually the long hours and unhappiness took their toll. Cyndi was discouraged and her vocal cords were damaged. She found a friend to take her place in the band, and in 1977 Cyndi left Flyer.

Cyndi has always been a dynamic performer —but until she began singing her own songs, something was missing.

The friend recommended a vocal coach to Cyndi—Katie Agresta, a Manhattan teacher who taught both classical and pop performers. Katie recognized the extraordinary range and quality in Cyndi's four-octave voice, but knew that she needed special training to bring out its full potential. Cyndi began to rebuild her voice and, once again, her belief in herself.

In a few months Cyndi felt ready to go to work again. Soon she was singing at a club in Manhattan called Trude Heller's. Her manager at the time, Ted Rosenblatt, introduced her to John Turi, a saxophonist and songwriter. Cyndi, John, and three other musicians formed a band called Blue Angel. Six months later the band signed with Polygram Records. Their first, and only album, *Blue Angel,* was released in 1980. Even though the critics liked *Blue Angel,* and especially Cyndi, critical acclaim was not enough. The album didn't sell.

*The cover of Blue Angel's
one and only album.
Cyndi, from the back cover
of the album*

The entire record business was in trouble in 1981. Sales were down. It was a time when no one wanted to take chances. The executives at Polygram wanted Cyndi to go solo, but she didn't want to break away from the band who had worked so hard with her. Polygram ended its contract with Blue Angel, and the band broke up.

It was a tough time for Cyndi, but she was no quitter. She took a series of odd jobs. She worked at a Japanese bar called Miho. She exercised horses at a New York race track. She sold antique clothes at a Manhattan boutique called Screaming Mimi's. At least she could still express herself by dressing up! Cyndi hung on.

Cyndi in Screaming Mimi's
—this time as a customer

Around this time, Cyndi met Dave Wolff, and began a personal and professional partnership which would, in a very short time, put Cyndi at the top of the charts. Dave was managing a band called ArcAngel, which was under contract with Portrait Records, a division of CBS. Dave took Cyndi to Portrait, and by the spring of 1983, Cyndi had a contract to record an album of her own.

Portrait assigned producer Rick Chertoff to the project, and Cyndi was involved in every aspect of the album, from cowriting songs to supervising the cover. *She's So Unusual* was released in October 1983.

As they were for *Blue Angel,* critical reviews of the new album were good. But no matter how good an album is, it needs publicity to make it big. Cyndi and Portrait Records gave *She's So Unusual* all their energy.

Cyndi with her boyfriend
and manager, Dave Wolff

By this time, music video had become a major force in the record industry, and was still growing. Watching cable television's Music Television channel (MTV), fans could now see, as well as hear, their favorite songs and stars. *She's So Unusual* was moving on the charts, but slowly, and a top-notch video would give the album the exposure it needed. Twenty-two-million MTV viewers would see her and hear her music. Cyndi brought in her friends Ken Walz and Edd Griles to shoot a video for ''Girls Just Want To Have Fun,'' a key song on *She's So Unusual.*

Cyndi with Edd Griles and Ken Walz on the set of ''Girls Just Want To Have Fun''

*Cyndi dancing in the streets
and (left) relaxing during a
lull in the shooting of "Girls"*

At last Cyndi had an outlet for all her creative energies. She contributed to every part of the video—the sets, costumes, choreography, and production. She called on friends, her Mom, Dave, her old pals from Ozone Park, even her dog, Sparkle, to appear with her in "Girls." Captain Lou Albano, a colorful character from the world of professional wrestling, played Cyndi's father. The video was pure Cyndi.

*Cyndi with Captain
Lou Albano in "Girls"*

Cyndi made "Girls" her song of joy and freedom, and the video shows Cyndi at her most energetic and exciting—dancing with her friends through the streets of New York, into her mother's kitchen, and right into her room for an all night party. The girls *were* having fun, and it was contagious. Audiences loved it. "Girls" quickly sold the million copies needed to earn a gold record, and *She's So Unusual* climbed to the Top Ten.

Cyndi and her entourage dancing through the streets of New York in "Girls"

Again with Walz and Griles, Cyndi did a video for "Time After Time," another cut from the album. It followed "Girls" as a smash MTV hit. In June, the third Walz/Griles video, "She Bop," followed, and Cyndi found herself in the astonishing position of having three hit videos on MTV, back to back. At last Cyndi Lauper was professionally visible, as a singer and a music video star.

Cyndi with Dave Wolff
on the set of "She Bop,"
her third smash video

Cyndi kept the momentum going. She was a guest on Johnny Carson's *Tonight Show*. She presented awards at the 1984 Grammys. She toured the country for fourteen weeks. In April she was nominated for "Best Female Performance" at the American Video Awards. Shortly afterward, her videos were nominated in eight categories for the First Annual MTV Video Awards. She was nominated as "Best New Artist" for both "Girls" and "Time After Time." Cyndi's toughest competition was herself!

Cyndi having fun with Johnny on The Tonight Show *and in concert in Los Angeles*

Also in the summer of 1984, Cyndi moved into yet another highly visible field, professional wrestling. Both pop music and wrestling are dramatic entertainment, peopled with outspoken and colorful characters. Professional wrestling programs are among the most popular shows on cable television, and MTV has its own enormous following. Putting the two together was too good to resist. It was a media marriage made in TV heaven.

Although they had worked together in three videos, Cyndi decided it was time to publicly confront the brash and bizarre Captain Lou Albano. It was quite a match! Cyndi has always been an outspoken feminist, and was outraged by Captain Lou's sexist remarks. The two began a much-publicized quarrel. Cyndi told the world she wouldn't let him get away with saying that women belonged in the kitchen!

Cyndi and longtime friend Captain Lou Albano decided to settle their differences in the ring.

She challenged Captain Lou to a showdown in the ring—a contest between a wrestler he managed, The Fabulous Moolah, who had held the Women's Wrestling Championship for over twenty-five years, and her arch-rival, wrestler Wendi Richter, whom Cyndi herself would manage for the fight.

Sponsored by CBS and MTV, and promoted by the World Wrestling Federation, the July 23 match drew a star-studded audience for its live broadcast from Madison Square Garden. Many thousands of fans watched the match on television sets across the country. Exuberantly cheered on by Cyndi and Captain Lou, Richter and The Moolah went at it. At the last moment, Richter scored an upset victory. Cyndi declared it a victory for all women over sexist thinking like Captain Lou's.

Cyndi with Wendi Richter, the wrestler she managed to victory over Captain Lou's Fabulous Moolah

The battle over, Cyndi and Captain Lou publicly made up, and served as cochairs for the 1984 Multiple Sclerosis Foundation fund drive. Directing their reunited energies toward the cause, they raised thousands of dollars for multiple sclerosis research.

In September, "Girls Just Want To Have Fun" was named "Best Female Video" at the MTV Video Awards, and *She's So Unusual* went platinum. Cyndi spent the last night of 1984 at a very appropriate party—MTV's Third Annual New Year's Eve Ball. She had a lot to celebrate, and she had earned it.

Cyndi at the MTV Video Awards, where "Girls Just Want To Have Fun" won the Best Female Video award

Early in 1985, Cyndi received five Grammy nominations, and won her first Grammy as "Best New Artist." Her videos were nominated for seven awards from the National Academy of Video Arts and Sciences (NAVAS), the Academy Awards of music videos. Cyndi collected six awards, including Best Pop Video for "Time After Time."

She was pictured on covers of *Newsweek* and *Life* as the symbol of the new creative female movement in pop music. *People* and *Us* wrote feature articles about her. *Ms.* magazine named Cyndi one of their 1984 women of the year, celebrating her as a feminist pop hero.

The awards came flooding in—
Cyndi with Geraldine Ferraro
and Gloria Steinem after being
named one of Ms. magazine's
1984 Women of the Year and
(over) with the two awards she
won at the American Music Awards.
After winning the Best New Artist
Grammy, Cyndi gets an added lift
from pro-wrestler friend Hulk Hogan.

Cyndi continued to work. She recorded the theme song "Good Enough" for Steven Spielberg's film *The Goonies*, and, of course, filmed a video to go with it. As always, Cyndi finds time to put her energies where her heart is. In an effort to provide relief to drought-starved Ethiopia, producer Quincy Jones brought together over forty American pop stars to contribute their talents to the USA for Africa Fund. Cyndi joined a galaxy of other superstars at the recording session, including Tina Turner, Ray Charles, Stevie Wonder, Bruce Springsteen, Diana Ross, and Bob Dylan. In a song called "We Are the World," written by Michael Jackson and Lionel Richie, each artist sings a short piece; Cyndi's voice soars strong and radiant, straight from the heart.

Cyndi with Bruce Springsteen at the historic recording session for "We Are the World"

Cyndi has come a long way from Ozone Park. The multitalented multimedia girl has found her place, and it is right at the top. She was gifted with an extraordinary and unstoppable talent, and she has nourished that talent with determination, imagination, and energy. Today, the orange-haired girl with the wacky clothes is recognized and honored as an artist, a feminist, and a champion of individuality and personal freedom. And Cyndi Lauper is still having fun!